CW01197405

THE VISIONS OF BEYA BEAN BLUE

The Visions of Beya Bean Blue

Written by: zO-AlonzO Gross

Illustrator: Salah Mezian

Seed Royale Publishing

CONTENTS

Dedication vii

1 - Meet Beya Bean Blue 1

2 - Jooky And Jack 3

3 - Swish, Swish Ricky The Fish 5

4 - Sister Lilly Jean Drew, Father Lou And The Zoo . . . 6

5 - Hey Hey Hey It's Blue Monster Ray 8

6 - Kalamazoo & The Ghost That Said "Boo". 10

7 - Blue Monsters In The Woods But It's All Good. . . 13

8 - Hold Your Head Remember What Grandpa Said . . 16

9 - Oh Snap! Just Like That Grandpa Is Back!. 18

10 - No Need For Cries, Blue Dog, New Roses, The Butterfly In Blue Skies. 19

11 - Beya Bean Blue & The Precious Child In You . . . 22

About The Author 25

Reviews 29

Beya Collage 35

"To the children of the world. May your Beautiful imaginations & Dreams take you to places you never thought possible. This is your time. Shine as Radiant as the lights at night that smile upon you in your precious slumber". zO-AlonzO Gross

Copyright © 2023 by zO-AlonzO Gross.
Written, Conceived, Co- Arranged & Co-Edited by: zO-AlonzO Gross.
Illustrated by Salah Mezian.
Edited & Arranged by Alexia Zakariya
Published by zO-AlonzO Gross & Alexia Zakariya for Seed Royale Publishing & Entertainment
2023 Books N Music We On It!

All rights reserved. No part of this book may be reproduced in any manner whatsoever without written permission except in the case of brief quotations embodied in critical articles and reviews.

First Printing, 2023

1

MEET BEYA BEAN BLUE

This is a story
About a Kid I knew,
I mean a real cool kid
They called him
Beya Bean Blue.

He always had
The best of dreams
Of his Monster friends
They made him feel
So glad
He didn't have to pretend.

2

JOOKY AND JACK

There was that one night
He dreamed about
Jooky & Jack
His two Monster friends
Who acted kind of cooky
In fact,

They liked to make
Funny sounds
As they growled
In the grass
And jump all around
Now that always makes
Beya Bean laugh.

3

SWISH, SWISH RICKY THE FISH

Beya Bean
Had another dream
Where he got whisked
Into a boat on a stream
Where he saw Ricky the Fish

He picked Ricky up
As the Monsters watched
In horror
"Beya, PLEASE!,
PLEASE, Beya!,
Put Ricky back in the water!"

4

SISTER LILLY JEAN DREW, FATHER LOU AND THE ZOO

Now Beya Bean Blue
Has a Sister who's two
Her name is
Lilly Jean Drew
She loves to eat cashews

Their Father named Lou
Works down the street
At the Zoo
He reads them really neat
Books on
Cockatoos and
Kangaroos.

5

HEY HEY HEY IT'S BLUE MONSTER RAY

Then, there was the day
Beya dreamed
Of a blue Monster
Named
Ray
With two big teeth
And huge eyes
Going every which way,

But he wasn't mean
Even as, "Grrrrr!"
Would he say
Blue Ray
Seemed to love to watch
The Moon
And Stars
Come to play.

6

KALAMAZOO & THE GHOST THAT SAID, "BOO".

Beya Bean Blue
When he visited
Kalamazoo
Became afraid but why?
He hadn't had a clue
All he knew
Is in the closet
Thought he heard a
Ghost say,
"Boo!"
Even though his Daddy
Lou
Said, "Beya that isn't
True."

Still under the covers
Beya hid
A frightened little kid
At 2.

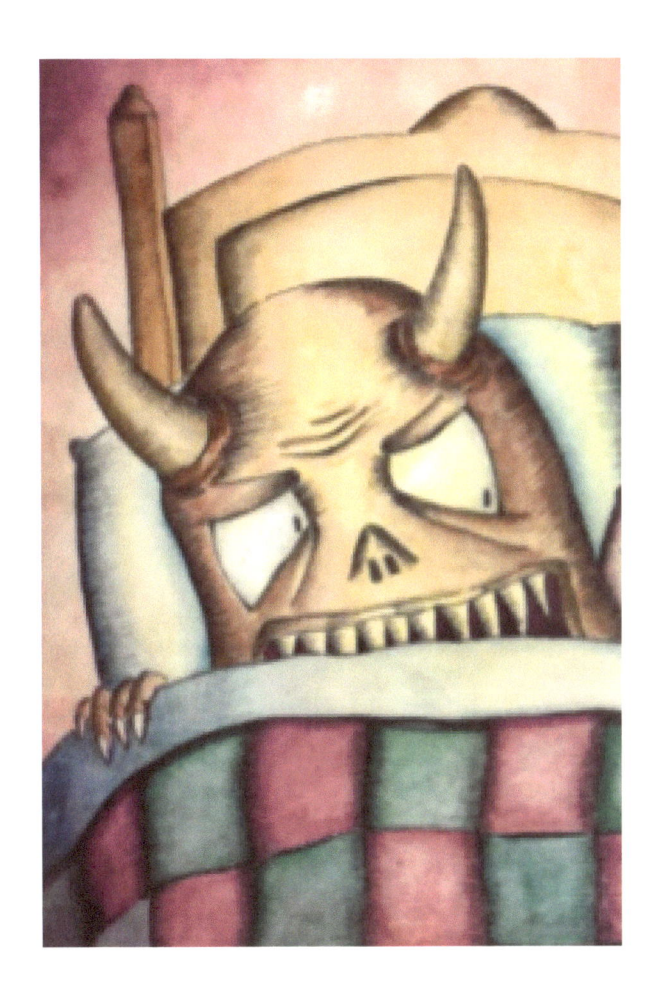

'Till his Monster
Friend Will
Thought, "Hey I know
What to do."

He said,
"Beya fear me not,
I will protect you as you
Lay
There's no Ghosts
But if there were trust me
I'd chase them all away."

"I have many Monster
Friends
We also love the color
Blue
They love me to no end,
And Brother Friend
They will love you too
Now there's a flower for
Your Ear
When you wear this I will
Appear."

Beya,
A smile upon his face
Felt fear just leave with
Not a trace.

7

BLUE MONSTERS IN THE WOODS BUT IT'S ALL GOOD.

Once Beya Bean Blue
Went Camping,
With Sister & Father Lou
He had a camera that he
Got from his Father's
Brother, Stew

It got late as they all fell
Asleep
In the tent,
That's exactly when he
Saw
His Monster friends
There were ten
"Oh", he thought to
Himself.
"What a magic event."

Standing at the top of
The hill,
There was Bill and Phil,
Amil and McGill
Mackenzie & Frenchy

Pam & Jan
& Nancy & Leslie.

Then Beya took out his
Camera
And said, "Can I take your
pic?" they said,
"Sure, we'd love that Beya
But please make it quick,
It sure looks like rain we
Don't want to get sick."
So Beya turned on his
Camera,
Flash!
And captured this flick.

8

HOLD YOUR HEAD REMEMBER WHAT GRANDPA SAID.

Then Beya Bean got
Some bad news the other
Day
His Grandfather Edgar
James
Suddenly passed away.

This was Beya's Father's
Dad,
And he felt so very sad
But he remembered a
Talk
He and his Grandfather
Had.

His Grandpa said, "Beya
One day you won't see
Me anymore,
But I will live on in your

Heart & Imagination for
Sure.
You and your Baby Sister
Will surely see me in dreams
And I

Will comfort you still
Like
The Blue River Streams."

"Beya, My Son, you don't
Have to cry for me, For I
Will visit you in whatever
Form you want me to be."

9

OH SNAP! JUST LIKE THAT GRANDPA IS BACK!.

Sure enough
Beya Bean had a dream
One June,
With his Baby Sister
And Grandpa Edgar in
Full Bloom.

There he was Grandpa
Just like he said,
Smiling with his cane
The Stars & Moon
Overhead.

Beya felt much joy
Seeing Grandpa again
That's when Grandpa
Said,
"Beya I sure love your
Monstrous Friends."

10

NO NEED FOR CRIES, BLUE DOG, NEW ROSES, THE BUTTERFLY IN BLUE SKIES.

An exciting dream that
Beya Bean had,
Was when he dreamt
He was a Blue Dog
Whose huge tail would
Wag.

But thinking of his
Granddad
He nearly began to cry
'Till a voice said, "Hey Lad
Don't be sad, it's me see
I'm the Butterfly."

Grinning from his soul
That Grandpa again was
Near,
He then noticed
The Beautiful Roses
That suddenly appeared.

"See I told you son,
No need to cry

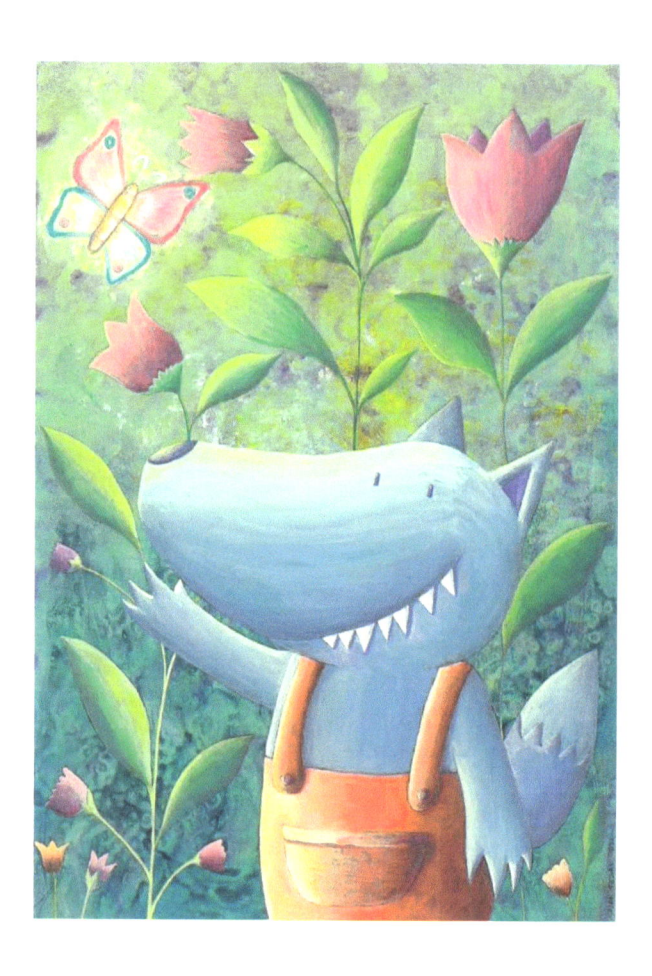

For my wings are one
With the gentle winds
The blossoming of Spring
And the lovely face
Of a childlike sky."

He went on to say
"Hey Burden not your heart in
Sorrows,
For I will send you Sunrise
For your Wondrous
Days of the Morrow."

Soaring high
Over the crescent bay away
With the birds,
Grandpa always had
Such a pleasant way
With words.

11

BEYA BEAN BLUE & THE PRECIOUS CHILD IN YOU

This was a story
About a Joy I knew
A Beautiful Boy
They called him
Beya Bean Blue.

Who had the fluffiest
Of dreams, Scenes
That danced in his mind
With his Imagination
Not a Mountain
He couldn't climb.

So if you have
A precious child
Who has a laugh
So free,
Let their spirit run wild
Like Joy
Yourself used to see.
Sleep with a smile & a
Grin.

That's when your
Innocence
Shows

Keep your Inner Child
Within
And may your
Love of Light grow

For our visions are our
Gifts
A Wind of Hope
When it blows

Once a Monster
Now a friend
Grandpa the Butterfly
Knows.
;-)

Photo by:
Alexia Zakariya

About the Author, zO-AlonZo Gross:

zO-AlonZo Gross is an American Rap Artist, Writer, Songwriter, Dancer, Actor, Producer, Composer, Publisher, Author and an International Multi-Award Winning Poet. In 2022 his 3rd book POEMZ 4 U AND YOURZ received : "1st place Poetry book of the Year at the Bookfest Book Awards of Los Angeles California, "1st place Poetry Book of the Year" (Urban Category) at the International Book Awards, "The 2022 Literary Excellence Award" at the Pen Craft Book Awards & A Finalist at the American Book Awards. Also, in 2022 zO received "The 2022 Golden Heart Literary Prize" awarded to him by the World Foundation.

His books include: "Inspiration, Harmony and the World Within" (2012) "Soul Elixir: The WritingZ of zO" (2018), "PoemZ 4 U and YourZ" (2021) & "the mc (The Meditative ContemplationZ) 2023. In addition, his works have appeared in numerous Anthologies including: the top selling Absolute Poetry Anthologies 1 & 2, (2021, 2022) he was featured in the Open Skies Anthology 2021 & Featured as a Global Poet in the Anthologies "The Year of The Poet book 1" & "The Year of the Poet book 2" in which he was recognized as one of the Best Poets in the World for 2021 & 2022. Most recently zO became the recipient of "The

2023" World Literary Award" in the category of Classical Literature representing the United States of America presented to him again by the World Foundation.

    zO is a graduate of Temple University with a Major in English Literature and a Minor in Dance. In 2021, he & his wife Singer, Songwriter & Author Alexia Zakariya also known as AZA started Seed Royale Publishing and look to publish other artists and writers. zO lives with his Wife and their 3 children in Pennsylvania.

Photo of:
Salah Mezian

About the Illustrator
Salah Mezian an Award Winning Illustrator
was born in Melilla on July 10, 1978. As a multidisciplinary artist, illustrator and writer, he develops multiple activities. Among others, artisan bookbinder, puppet maker, graphic designer and, above all, children's illustrator, an aspect that occupies an imprint of the artistic discipline he addresses. But where to stand out among all these artistic disciplines is children's illustration. Self-taught since his beginnings in the world of art, his work is closely related to dreams, populated by monsters, anthropomorphic characters, trips to fantastic worlds, etc.
In his works he tries to capture a universe traveled by the coordinates of fantasy. That lodges the limitless imagination of the little readers. To do this, he uses different techniques combined with recycled materials, thus

achieving the desired drawing and textual and graphic materialization of dreams.
Within his artistic activity, he has carried out several exhibitions of children's illustrations in the cities of Melilla, Madrid, Málaga and Córdoba. Some of his works are exhibited in the art gallery "Amused Fine art and extraordinary books" in Texas (USA). He currently works in his hometown, as coordinator of the NGO "Fundación Mensajeros de la Paz"

REVIEWS

'The Visions of Beya Bean Blue' by zO-AlonzO Gross is a sweet, series of poems that focus on the dreams, and life-experiences of a young boy. The poems display the simplicity and joy of a child's imagination, and handles sensitive topics, such as nightmares of monsters that become friends in a way a child would appreciate, and the death of the young boy's grandfather handled with tact, and a tangibility that consoles and comforts.

In addition, the illustrations by Selah Mezian are simple yet colorful and blend well with the poems. A Beautiful children's book from an acclaimed poet."

-William- Gensburger,
Best-selling Author of 'Texas Dead".
CEO of Books N Pieces Magazine.

zo-AlonzO Gross is a Multi-talented dancer, writer, rap artist, compose, producer, actor, poet, and Multi Award winning published author who has written a most remarkable modern day classic children's book Inspired by his son Beya Prince Gross.

As in his previous books, zO's ability to create sound patterns with his words makes reading this book a joy for children and adults alike. The theme of facing one's monsters with friendliness instead of fear is empowering to children, and zO is able to communicate this theme in a way that is both whimsical and fun.

The book is beautifully illustrated by Salah Mezian in a style reminiscent of Maurice Sendak (Where the Wild Things Are), with drawings designed to unlock the power of dreams and imagination within the child.

This book also touches on death in a gentle and loving way with the hopeful promise that those departed are still around us. I find myself fascinated by this book and every time I re-read it I find new delights to make me smile. A must read for all children young and old!

-Arlene Schar, 72
Violinist. Chef

I have read many Beautiful poems by zO and regard him a perfect poet with his lyrical note and poignant expressions. I had no idea that he would write such a fabulous book for young children!

The Visions of Beya Bean Blue is a sweet poetic tale. zO, as a magician, comes with a bewitching tale for young children. I was greatly awed by this artistic and fascinating graphic poetic tale. Based on visions and imagination, as if a prophet would be unfolding the story.

This children's book is based on the perspective of a boy who is blessed with innocence, love, beauty, and companionship. The boy, Beya Bean Blue, goes beyond a common thread of human understanding that monsters are evils and harmful. He proves that they are not so in fanciful world of the children! It means power of innocence and imagination that children bear in their lives do wonders. Long time ago, the great romantic and visionary poet William Blake, did say that the songs of innocence are beauty of life, as they are songs not heard by many and become universal songs to last for century. In the same vein, Beya befriends with the monster and they both make a bond that there is nothing wrong in life. As their hearts are pure and immaculate, they don't see any distinction between them and even the world around them. They are meek and innocent like the lambs in the pastures which don't run even they see the wolves!

Furthermore, the book is a perfect piece in terms of its illustration, and the child friendly theme. The language is nicely culled to make it suitable for the children. The color combinations and the moods of the pictures manifest are tuned to its thematic intent.

This is the perfect book to be used for class purposes regardless of the level of education solely based on the deeply enriching themes that permeate within this story made for children & their parents to enjoy. A Modern Day Classic.

Bam Dev Sharma
Writer, Poet & Author
Tribhuwan University, R.R College
English Department
Exhibition Road, Kathmandu
Nepal
Author of :

The Shepherd in the Sky (A collection of children's stories)
The Magician and the Fairy (A children's novel)
Finding God (Moral stories for young children)
The Wise Shepherd (A collection of the children's stories)

zO -Artfully and Imaginatively captures a universal message. Monsters and all else are not to be feared. When anything frightful is brought under the power of our dreams and imaginations, it can become beautiful and even nurturing. With the power of our minds, we can learn from childhood onwards that our loved ones are forever near, and there is nothing under the bed to fear. When dealing with weighty matters such as losing loved ones or facing the unknown, the book through the power of dreams addresses life with whimsy and hope. Beya Bean Blue is a truly wonderful and transformative read!

-Monica Marie Eimad Zakariya
Teacher/Writer/Poet/Author
Chicago

From the pen of the multi-talented zO-AlonzO Gross, this heart-warming and delightful story takes us into the magical world of Beya Bean Blue. Accompanied with beautiful artwork, we are welcomed on this special journey of a little boy as he navigates his fantastical world.

   The Visions of Beya Bean Blue brings not only humor, but gentle lessons in life...from bereavement to fear to nurturing our own inner creative worlds.

With whimsical poetic language and flowing rhymes, this is a book that all can enjoy and share...with not only the children in our lives, but also the ones we carry within ourselves.

- Lucie Sargeant (Poet, author and social media collaborator.) UK

BEYA COLLAGE

Photo of:
Beya Prince Gross

To our baby boy Beya Prince Gross
Daddy & Mommy Love you with every fiber of our very being.

Ingram Content Group UK Ltd.
Milton Keynes UK
UKHW052154190323
418780UK00003B/11